Thai Phrasebook
1,001

Learn Thai Language for Beginners

1,001 Easy to Learn Thai Phrases

SAENCHAI GLORY

Copyright 2016 - All Rights Reserved – *SAENCHAI GLORY*
ALL RIGHTS RESERVED. No part of this publication may be reproduced or transmitted in any form whatsoever, electronic, or mechanical, including photocopying, recording, or by any informational storage or retrieval system without express written, dated and signed permission from the author.

Table of Contents

INTRODUCTION	5
NUMBERS – ตัวเลข – (TUA-LEK)	11
TIME AND DATE – วันและเวลา – WAN-LAE-WE-LA	20
FAMILY – ครอบครัว (KHROP-KHRUA)	33
DIRECTIONS – ทิศทาง	43
GREETINGS – ทักทาย – (THAK-THAI)	51
JOBS & EDUCATION – อาชีพและการศึกษา – A-CHIP-LAE-KAN-SUEK-SA	57
HOTELS & LODGING – โรงแรมและที่พักชั่วคราว – RONG-RAEM-LAE-THI-PHAK- CHUA-KHRAO	74
FEELINGS – ความรู้สึก – KHWAM-RU-SUEK	88
EATING, DRINKING, & NIGHTLIFE – กิน ดื่ม เที่ยวกลางคืน – KIN-DUEM-THIAO-KLANG-KHUEN	99
HOBBIES & SPORTS – งานอดิเรกและกีฬา – NGAN-A-DI-REK-LAE-KI-LA	125
COMMON QUESTIONS & ANSWERS – คำถามและคำตอบทั่วๆไป – KHAM-THAM LAE-KHAM-TOP-THUA-THUA-PAI	136
REACTING TO GOOD NEWS – การตอบสนองต่อข่าวดี – KAN-TOP-SA-NONG-TO- KHAO-DI	152
WHAT ARE YOU DOING? – คุณกำลังทำอะไร – KHUN-KAM-LANG-THAM-A-RAI	159
CLOTHING & APPEARANCE – เครื่องแต่งกายและรูปลักษณ์ภายนอก - KHRUEANG-TAENG-KAI-LAE-RUP-LAK-PHAI-NOK	161
PROBLEM SOLVING – จัดการปัญหา – CHAT-KAN-PAN-HA	175
THE BODY – ร่างกาย	179

AIRPLANES & AIRPORTS – เครื่องบินและสนามบิน – KHRUEANG-BIN-LAE-SA-NAM-BIN 188

SENTENCE STARTERS – การเริ่มประโยค – KHAN-ROEM-PRA-YOK 195

SHOPPING & NEGOTIATING – การซื้อของและการต่อรอง – KAN-SUE-KHONG-LAE- KAN-TO-RONG 199

DATING & PERSONAL – การเดท และ เรื่องของบุคคล – KAN-DET-LAE-RUEANG –KHONG-BUK-KHON 205

CONCLUSION 218

Introduction

Thailand is perhaps unique among many Southeast Asian countries in the way it straddles its Eastern roots with Western influences.

Unlike many of its neighbors it has never really been conquered or occupied. To the east you come against Myanmar and the remnants of the British raj. To the north you find China which has alternated largely between influences of British colonialism around Hong Kong or quite severe cultural isolation. To the east you find Cambodia, Laos, and Vietnam which felt the presence of the USA very heavily from the 40s to the 60s.

These influences passed through Thailand yet they didn't take hold in the same way, although they weren't rejected either.

There is never any doubt when you are in Thailand that you are experiencing a truly unique Asian culture, but it has also happily taken in many of the freedoms and conveniences the Western world has to offer. It manages to create a fusion of culture that feels vibrant and modern while still being honest to its ancient ways and customs.

Thanks to this Thailand has become the expat capital of Southeast Asia as it offers the comfort and ease of living Westerners crave, but also the warmth and happiness that characterizes many Buddhist cultures. This combined with the low cost of living, the ease of moving here, the ideal tropical climate, and the perfect mixture of gorgeous beaches, lush jungle, and sprawling neon-lit cities makes it one of the most enticing places for those looking to relocate.

Not only are people coming to live in Thailand in big numbers but the tourist industry is booming. The World Tourism Organization ranked it as ninth in the world for tourism and Bangkok was ranked the fourth most visited city in the world with 16 million people visiting a year. The only cities above it were the two city states of Hong Kong and Singapore, and London.

With all these visitors you might think that speaking Thai might be optional when it comes to getting by in Thailand, but this is not entirely accurate. Reportedly 27% of Thailand's population (17 million people) speaks English which is higher than many of its neighboring countries; however the numbers don't paint a perfect picture.

Thai people that have studied at university will almost certainly have some English, as do many people many business people and those that deal directly with tourists, yet you'll find that it can be limited and English speakers are often isolated to the cities and even there to the more educated citizens.

If you want to tell a taxi driver where you want to go in English you're going to need to have it written down unless it's a popular tourist destination. If you speak only English haggling will usually involve lots of pointing and the holding up of fingers. Of the 17 million English speakers many would be better described as English readers, because their spoken English can leave something to the imagination.

All this means that if you want to get by in Thailand you either teach everyone English as you go, or you learn some basic Thai. And with it being such a fascinating and beautiful language, why wouldn't you want to?

The Thai language is often split into Northern, Central, and Southern Thai, which are separate languages spoken in their respective parts of the country, but there is a lot of crossover and nearly all Thai people can more-or-less easily communicate with each other. The most common form, and the one that will usually just be called 'Thai', is Central Thai.

Around Thailand many people speak different languages or very different variations of Thai. In the north you might find people speaking Isaan, or Lao, and around the borders of the country you might find people speaking Khmer. In the hill villages you will a wide range of different languages spoken, although many will still speak some Thai.

Thai is what is known as a tonal language which means that the pitch you say a word with (high, middle, or low) can change the meaning of a word. The different tones used in Thai can be very subtle for foreign people to pick up and if you take learning the language more seriously the fun will come from saying the different words just right. Learning these tones won't just be a matter of learning new sounds but maybe even learning whole new ways of moving your mouth.

Because of this tonality there are different variants of spoke Thai across the country, but nearly everyone uses a form of Central Thai to write with. In general people will use central Thai for school and work, and then use either central Thai or their regional variation on the language at home.

You don't need to worry about the tones if you are just learning phrases, however, this guide will help you compensate for the difference, and local Thai people will understand you are not a native speaker and will adjust how they listen to you speaking Thai. It's only if you want to have a more sophisticated grasp of Thai that you will need to focus on tones.

More difficult than actually learning to speak and get-by with Thai, is learning how to write and read the language. There are over 50 different letters within the Thai alphabet, but they are not quite letters as we know them in English as not all the consonants or vowels are usable on their own.

This may sound contradictory but Thai is quite a simple language, and this simplicity makes it harder to learn as a lot can be said with a little, and you have to decipher quite bit of nuance into the language to read it fluently.

Luckily many signs in Thailand are also written out in English and you will be fine just learning how to speak phrases.

Thai is spoken mostly in Thailand and between 50 and 60 million people speak the Central Thai version of it, with 20 million of them having it as a primary language spoken in the home. Thailand has a population of 67 million – so basically everyone you meet will speak Thai in Thailand. There are few Thai speakers outside of Thailand but neighboring languages have many similarities to Thai.

You will often hear that locals in various countries like it when you attempt to speak their language and it doesn't always seem to be the case in practice, but in Thailand you'll find not only will locals love it, but you'll have fun trying to use different phrases. Although many Thai people will revert to English if they can speak it as they are usually trying to help you out.

Thailand is a very friendly nation that prides itself on politeness. This means that people will often try to chat with you and the simple effort to show respect to someone in their language will mean a great deal to them.

The politeness here isn't deferential as it might seem in some other Asian languages with specific ways of speaking to those perceived to be above you. Instead politeness in language applies to everyone and is given as a sign of warmth: even more so than in English in some cases.

If you spend enough time speaking to and trading stories with Thai people you might notice that things such as sarcasm don't feature as heavily in the language. You might even find that some of the more abrasive or rude aspects of language that are commonly found in English do not go down as well among Thai people. This is not to say they cannot take a joke, just that there is a slightly different cultural perception about what is funny which leans more towards wordplay.

To get the most out of your time in Thailand you will need to try and pick up a few phrases and to really test them out in different and exciting situations. This isn't just because it's the friendly thing to do, but without certain phrases you will be stuck on the usual tourist path.

Whenever you ask a local for help in English they will just have to send you along to the safest and most tourist friendly thing they can think of. Learn the language a little though, and you open up a whole new bunch of doors with rich experiences that only a local can show you.

As you go through this phrase book remember to have fun and accept that you are a complete beginner. Define your goals so that you won't be disappointed if you don't progress as quickly as you anticipated.

The phrases here can be used on a daily basis when you are in Thailand and you shouldn't have any fear trying them out once you're there. Take every opportunity you can to use your new Thai phrases and express your love for this beautiful country.

Numbers – ตัวเลข – (Tua-lek)

One

หนึ่ง

(nueng)

Two

สอง

(song)

Three

สาม

(sam)

Four

สี่

(si)

Five

ห้า

(ha)

Six

หก

(hok)

Seven

เจ็ด

(chet)

Eight

แปด

(paed)

Nine

เก้า

(kao)

Ten

สิบ

(sip)

Eleven

สิบเอ็ด

(sip-ed)

Twelve

สิบสอง

(sip-song)

Thirteen

สิบสาม

(sip-sam)

Fourteen

สิบสี่

(sip-si)

Fifteen

สิบห้า

(sip-ha)

Sixteen

สิบหก

(sip-hok)

Seventeen

สิบเจ็ด

(sip-chet)

Eighteen

สิบแปด

(sip-paed)

Nineteen

สิบเก้า

(sip-kao)

Twenty

ยี่สิบ

(yi-sip)

Thirty

สามสิบ

(sam-sip)

Forty

สี่สิบ

(si-sip)

Fifty

ห้าสิบ

(ha-sip)

Sixty

หกสิบ

(hok-sip)

Seventy

เจ็ดสิบ

(jed-sip)

Eighty

แปดสิบ

(paed-sip)

Ninety

เก้าสิบ

(kao-sip)

One hundred

หนึ่งร้อย

(nueng-roi)

Two hundred

สองร้อย

(song-roi)

Five Hundred

ห้าร้อย

(ha-roi)

One thousand

หนึ่งพัน

(neung-pun)

Five thousand

ห้าพัน

(ha-pun)

One million (1M)

หนึ่งล้าน

(neung-lan)

Ten million

สิบล้าน

(sip-lan)

One billion (1000M)

หนึ่งพันล้าน

(neung-pun-lan)

One trillion (1,000,000M)

หนึ่งล้านล้าน

(neung-lan-lan)

How many do you have?

คุณมีเท่าไร

(*kun-me-tao-rai*)

Various

หลากหลาย

(lark-lhai)

Lots/A lot

มาก

(mak)

More

มากกว่า

(*mak-kwa*)

Less

น้อยกว่า

(noi-kwa)

Time and Date – วันและเวลา – wan-lae-we-la

What is the date?
วันที่เท่าไร

(wan-tee-tao-rai)

What day is today?
วันนี้วันอะไร

(wan-ni-wan-arai)

Monday
วันจันทร์

(wan-chan)

Tuesday
วันอังคาร

(wan-ang-khan)

Wednesday

วันพุธ

(wan-phut)

Thursday

วันพฤหัสบดี

(wan-pha-rue-hat-sa-bo-di)

Friday

วันศุกร์

(wan-suk)

Saturday

วันเสาร์

(wan-sao)

Sunday

วันอาทิตย์

(wan-ar-thit)

January

มกราคม

(mok-ka-ra-khom)

February

กุมภาพันธ์

(kum-pha-phan)

March

มีนาคม

(mi-na-khom)

April

เมษายน

(me-sa-yon)

May

พฤษภาคม

(phruet-sa-pha-khom)

June

มิถุนายน

(mi-thu-na-yon)

July

กรกฎาคม

(ka-rak-ka-da-khom)

August

สิงหาคม

(sing-ha-khom)

September

กันยายน

(Kan-ya-yon)

October

ตุลาคม

(Tu-la-khom)

November

พฤศจิกายน

(Phruet-sa-chi-ka-yon)

December

ธันวาคม

(Tan-wa-khom)

Next weekend

สุดสัปดาห์ถัดไป

(Sut-sapda-tat-pai)

Two weeks from now

สองสัปดาห์ถัดไป

(Song-sapda-tat-pai)

Next week

สัปดาห์หน้า

(Sapda-na)

Last week

สัปดาห์ที่แล้ว

(Sapda-thi-laeo)

During the week

ระหว่างสัปดาห์

(Ra-wang-sapda)

Weekend

สุดสัปดาห์

(Sut-sapda)

What time is it?

ตอนนี้กี่โมง

(Tonni-ki-mong)

It is 3:30PM

ตอนนี้บ่ายสามโมงครึ่ง

(Tonni-bai-sam-mong-khrueng)

One hour

หนึ่งชั่วโมง

(Nueng-chuamong)

Half hour

ครึ่งชั่วโมง

(Khrueng-chuamong)

What time?

ตอนไหน

(Ton-nai)

When

เมื่อไร

(*Muea-rai*)

Season

ฤดู

(Ruedu)

Fall

ฤดูใบไม้ร่วง

(Ruedu-baimai-ruang)

Winter

ฤดูหนาว

(Ruedu-nao)

Spring

ฤดูใบไม้ผลิ

(Ruedu-baimai-phli)

Summer

ฤดูร้อน

(Ruedu-ron)

Morning

เช้า

(Chao)

Afternoon

บ่าย

(Bai)

Day

กลางวัน

(*Klang-wan*)

Night/Evening

กลางคืน/เย็น

(Klang-khuen/Yen)

Last night

เมื่อคืน

(Muea-khuen)

Dawn

รุ่งอรุณ

(Rung-arun)

Dusk

ค่ำ

(Kham)

Early

ก่อน

(Kon)

Soon

ในไม่ช้า

(Nai-mai-cha)

Before

ก่อน

(kon)

Late

สาย

(sai)

Later

หลัง

(lang)

In the morning

ในตอนเช้า

(Nai-ton-chao)

In the afternoon

ในตอนบ่าย

(Nai-ton-bai)

In the evening

ในตอนเย็น

(Nai-ton-yen)

At what time?

ตอนกี่โมง

(Ton-ki-mong)

Since when?

ตั้งแต่เมื่อไร

(Tang-tae-muea-rai)

For three years

ตั้งสามปีแล้ว

(Tang-sam-pi-laeo)

One hour ago

ชั่วโมงที่แล้ว

(Chua-mong-thi-laeo)

A second

วินาที

(Wi-na-thi)

A minute

นาที

(Na-thi)

Noon

เที่ยง

(Thiang)

Midnight

เที่ยงคืน

(Thiang-khuen)

Family – ครอบครัว (khrop-khrua)

This is my family

นี่คือครอบครัวของฉัน

(ni-khue-khrop-khrua-khong-chan)

Father

คุณพ่อ

(khun-pho)

Dad

พ่อ

(pho)

Mother

คุณแม่

(khun-mae)

Mom

แม่

(mae)

Brother

พี่ชาย/น้องชาย

(Phi-chai/ Nong-chai)

Sister

พี่สาว/น้องสาว

(Phi-sao/ Nong-sao)

Siblings

พี่น้อง

(Phi-nong)

We're siblings

เราเป็นพี่น้องกัน

(Rao-pen-phi-nong-kan)

Cousin

ลูกพี่ลูกน้อง

(Luk-phi-luk-nong)

We're cousins

เราเป็นลูกพี่ลูกน้องกัน

(Rao-pen-luk-phi-luk-nong-kan)

Uncle

อา

(*ar*)

Aunt

ป้า

(*pa*)

Grandfather of my Mother

ตา

(ta)

Grandmother or my Mother

ยาย

(yai)

Grandfather of my Father

ปู่

(pu)

Grandmother of my Father

ย่า

(ya)

In-laws

ญาติโดยการสมรส

(Yat-doi-kan-somrot)

Father-in-law

พ่อตา

(Pho-ta)

Mother-in-law

แม่ยาย

(Mae-yai)

Brother-in-law

พี่เขย/น้องเขย

(Phi-khoei/Nong-khoei)

Sister-in-law

พี่สะใภ้/น้องสะใภ้

(Phi-sa-phai/nong-sa-phai)

Son-in-law

ลูกเขย

(Luk-khoei)

Daughter-in-law

ลูกสะใภ้

(Luk-sa-phai)

Stepfather

พ่อบุญธรรม

(Pho-bun-tham)

Stepmother

แม่บุญธรรม

(Mae-bun-tham)

Stepbrother

พี่ชายบุญธรรม/น้องชายบุญธรรม

(Phi-chai-bun-tham / Nong-chai-bun-tham)

Stepsister

พี่สาวบุญธรรม/น้องสาวบุญธรรม

(Phi-sao-bun-tham/Nong-sao-bun-tham)

Son

ลูกชาย

(Luk-chai)

Daughter

ลูกสาว

(Luk-sao)

Grandson

หลานชาย

(Lan–chai)

Granddaughter

หลานสาว

(Lan-sao)

Stepson

ลูกชายบุญธรรม

(Luk-chai-bun-tham)

Stepdaughter

ลูกสาวบุญธรรม

(Luk-sao-bun-tham)

Nephew

หลานชาย

(Lan–chai)

Niece

หลานสาว

(Lan-sao)

Boyfriend

แฟนชาย

(Faen-chai)

Girlfriend

แฟนสาว

(Faen-sao)

Child

ลูก

(Luk)

Identical twin brother

พี่ชายฝาแฝด/น้องชายฝาแฝด

(Phi-chai-fa-faet / Nong-chai-fa-faet)

Identical twin sister

พี่สาวฝาแฝด/น้องสาวฝาแฝด

(Phi-sao-fa-faet / Nong-sao-fa-faet)

Twin brother

พี่ชายฝาแฝด/น้องชายฝาแฝด

(Phi-chai-fa-faet / Nong-chai-fa-faet)

Twin sister

พี่สาวฝาแฝด/น้องสาวฝาแฝด

(Phi-sao-fa-faet / Nong-sao-fa-faet)

Godfather

พ่ออุปถัมป์

(Pho-U-Patham)

Godmother

แม่อุปถัมป์

(Mae-U-Patham)

Husband

สามี

(Sa-mi)

Wife

ภรรยา

(Phan-ya)

Relatives

ญาติ

(Yat)

How many siblings do you have?

คุณมีพี่น้องกี่คน

(*Khun-mi-phi-nong-ki-khon*)

Thai Phrase Book 1,001

Directions – ทิศทาง

Where
ที่ไหน

(*Thi-nai*)

Where is it?
มันอยู่ที่ไหน

(*Man-yu-thi-nai*)

Where is the hotel?
โรงแรมอยู่ที่ไหน

(rong-raem-yu-thi-nai)

Where is the subway?
รถไฟใต้ดินอยู่ที่ไหน

(*Rot-fai-tai-din-yu-thi-nai*)

Where is the bus?

รถเมล์อยู่ที่ไหน

(Rot-me-yu-thi-nai)

Where are the taxis?

รถแท็กซี่อยู่ที่ไหน

(*Rot-thaek-si-yu-thi-nai*)

What is the address?

ที่อยู่อะไร

(*Thi-yu-a-rai*)

How do I get to...

ฉันจะไป....ยังไง

(Chan-cha-pai ... . Yang-ngai)

Do you have a map?

คุณมีแผนที่ไหม

(Khun-mi-phaen-thi-mai)

Is it near?

มันใกล้ไหม

(Man-klai-mai)

Is it far?

มันไกลไหม

(Man-kai-mai)

Go back

กลับไป

(Klap-pai)

Follow

ตาม

(Tam)

Cross

ข้าม

(Kham)

Toward

ไปสู่

(Pai-su)

Straight

ตรง

(Trong)

Left

ซ้าย

(Sai)

Right

ขวา

(Khwa)

Near

ใกล้

(Klai)

Far

ไกล

(Kai)

Go up

ขึ้น

(Khuen)

Go down

ลง

(Long)

Up

ขึ้น

(Khuen)

Down

ลง

(Long)

Behind

ข้างหลัง

(Khang-lang)

In front of

ข้างหน้า

(Khang-na)

Go straight

ตรงไป

(Trong-pai)

Go that way

ไปทางนั้น

(Pai-thang-nan)

Turn right

เลี้ยวขวา

(Liao-khwa)

Turn left

เลี้ยวซ้าย

(Liao-sai)

Drop me off here, please

ขอลงตรงนี้

(*Kho-long-trong-ni*)

To walk

เดิน

(Doen)

To walk

เดิน

(Doen)

To drive

ขับรถ

(Khap-rot)

Street

ถนน

(Tha-non)

Highway

ทางหลวง

(Thang-luang)

Roundabout

อ้อม

(Om)

Corner

หัวมุม

(Hua-mum)

The next Street

ถนนถัดไป

(Tha-non-that-pai)

Greetings – ทักทาย – (Thak-Thai)

Hello

สวัสดี

(Sa-wat-di)

Good morning

อรุณสวัสดิ์

(A-run-sa-wat)

Good afternoon

ทิวาสวัสดิ์

(Thi-wa-sa-wat)

Good evening

สายัณห์สวัสดิ์

(Sa-yan-sa-wat)

How are you?

เป็นไงบ้าง

(Pen-ngai-bang)

Fine

สบายดี

(Sa-bai-di)

Very well

ดีมาก

(Di-mak)

So-so

งั้นๆ

(*Ngan-ngan*)

How's it going?

เป็นไงบ้าง

(Pen-ngai-bang)

How is everything?

เป็นไงบ้าง

(Pen-ngai-bang)

What's your name?

คุณชื่ออะไร

(*Khun-chue-a-rai*)

What is his/her name?

เขา/เธอ ชื่อว่าอะไร

(*Khao/ Thoe -Chue-wa-a-rai*)

My name is...

ฉันชื่อ ....

(Chan-chue ....)

I'm David

ฉันชื่อเดวิด

(Chan-chue-David)

Nice to meet you

ดีใจที่ได้เจอ

(Di-chai-thi-dai-choe)

Pleasure to meet you

ยินดีที่ได้รู้จัก

(Yin-di-thi-dai-ru-chak)

Goodbye

ลาก่อน

(La-kon)

Have a good day

ขอให้โชคดี

(Kho-hai-chok-di)

See you soon

เจอกัน

(choe-kan)

See you later

เจอกัน

(choe-kan)

See you tomorrow

เจอกันพรุ่งนี้

(choe-kan-phrung-ni)

Goodnight

ราตรีสวัสดิ์

(Ra-tri-sa-wat)

Where do you live?

คุณพักอยู่ไหน

(*Khun-phak-yu-nai*)

I live in...

ฉันพักอยู่ที่...

(Chan-phak-yu-thi...)

Where are you from?

คุณมาจากไหน

(Khun-ma-chak-nai)

I am from the United States

ฉันมาจากสหรัฐอเมริกา

(Chan-ma-chak-sa-ha-rat-America)

This is my friend

นี่เพื่อนของฉัน

(Ni-phuean-khong-chan)

Come with me

มากับฉัน

(Ma-kap-chan)

I had a wonderful time

ฉันมีช่วงเวลาที่แสนวิเศษ

(Chan-mi-chuang-we-la-thi-saen-wi-set)

Jobs & Education – อาชีพและการศึกษา – A-chip-lae-kan-suek-sa

To work

ทำงาน

(Tham-ngan)

I have to go to work

ฉันต้องไปทำงาน

(Chan-tong-pai-tham-ngan)

What do you do?

คุณทำอาชีพอะไร

(Khun-tham-a-chip-a-rai)

I work for...

ฉันทำงานให้...

(Chan-tham-ngan-hai)

Where do you work?

คุณทำงานที่ไหน

(Khun-tham-ngan-thi-nai)

I work in advertising

ฉันทำงานโฆษณา

(Chan-tham-ngan-kho-sa-na)

Career

อาชีพ

(a-chip)

Office

สำนักงาน

(Sam-nak-ngan)

Firm

บริษัท

(Bo-ri-sat)

Office park

พื้นที่สำนักงาน

(Phuen-thi-sam-nak-ngan)

Co-worker

เพื่อนร่วมงาน

(Phuean-ruam-ngan)

Colleague

เพื่อนร่วมงาน

(Phuean-ruam-ngan)

Business partner

หุ้นส่วนธุรกิจ

(Hun-suan-thu-ra-kit)

Company

บริษัท

(Bo-ri-sat)

Enterprise

วิสาหกิจ

(Wi-sa-ha-kit)

Business

ธุรกิจ

(Thu-ra-kit)

Agreement

ข้อตกลง

(Kho-tok-long)

Contract

สัญญา

(San-ya)

To hire

จ้าง

(Chang)

They hired me

พวกเขารับฉันเข้าทำงาน

(Phuak-khao-rap-chan-khao-tham-ngan)

Interview

สัมภาษณ์

(Sam-phat)

Employee

พนักงาน

(Pha-nak-ngan)

Boss

หัวหน้า

(Hua-na)

Executive

ผู้บริหาร

(Phu-bo-ri-han)

Employment

การจ้างงาน

(Kan-chang-ngan)

Staff

พนักงาน

(Pha-nak-ngan)

Job offer

ข้อเสนองาน

(Kho-sa-noe-ngan)

Training

การฝึก

(Kan-fuek)

Engineer

วิศวกร

(Wit-sa-wa-kon)

Scientist

นักวิทยาศาสตร์

(Nak-wit-tha-ya-sat)

Doctor (medical)

หมอ

(*Mo*)

Schedule a doctor visit

นัดพบหมอ

(Nat-phop-mo)

Lawyer

นักกฎหมาย

(Nak-kot-mai)

Police officer

ตำรวจ

(Tam-ruat)

Teacher

ครู

(Khru)

Journalist

นักข่าว

(Nak-khao)

Intern

เด็กฝึกงาน

(Dek-fuek-ngan)

Businessman

นักธุรกิจ

(Nak-thu-ra-kit)

Entrepreneur

ผู้ประกอบการ

(Phu-pra-kop-kan)

Owner
เจ้าของ

(Chao-khong)

Freelance
อาชีพอิสระ

(A-chip-it-sa-ra)

Study
เรียน

(Rian)

University
มหาวิทยาลัย

(Ma-ha-wit-tha-ya-lai)

Primary school
โรงเรียนประถม

(Rong-rian-pra-thom)

High school

โรงเรียนมัธยม

(Rong-rian-mat-tha-yom)

Subject

วิชา

(wi-cha)

Faculty

คณะ

(kah-na)

Degree

ปริญญา

(pa-rin-ya)

Studies

เรียน

(Rian)

Class

ชั้นเรียน

(Chan-rian)

Exam

สอบ

(Sop)

Grade

คะแนน

(Kha-naen)

What do you study?

คุณเรียนอะไร

(Khun-rian-a-rai)

What did you study?

คุณเรียนอะไรมา

(Khun-rian-a-rai-ma)

I study at the university

ฉันเรียนที่มหาวิทยาลัย

(Chan-rian-thi-ma-ha-wit-tha-ya-lai)

I am studying biology

ฉันเรียนเกี่ยวกับชีววิทยา

(Chan-rian-kiao-kap-chi-wa-wit-tha-ya)

Postgraduate degree

ระดับสูงกว่าปริญญาตรี

(Ra-dap-sung-kwa-pa-rin-ya-tri)

Master's degree

ปริญญาโท

(Pa-rin-ya-tho)

I am getting a master's degree in education

ฉันกำลังเรียนปริญญาโทคณะครุศาสตร์

(Chan-kam-lang-rian-pa-rin-ya-tho-kha-na-kha-ru-sat)

Course

หลักสูตร

(Lak-sut)

I am taking a business course

ฉันกำลังเรียนหลักสูตรธุรกิจ

(Chan-kam-lang-rian-lak-sut-thu-ra-kit)

We are studying hard

เรากำลังเรียนอย่างหนัก

(Rao-kam-lang-rian-yang-nak)

Semester

เทอม

(Term)

Lesson

บทเรียน

(Bot-rian)

Student

นักเรียน

(Nak-rian)

Doctorate

ปริญญาเอก

(Pa-rin-ya-ek)

Thesis

วิทยานิพนจ์

(Wit-tha-ya-ni-pon)

I get good grades

ฉันได้คะแนนดี

(Chan-dai-kha-naen-di)

Classmate

เพื่อนร่วมชั้น

(Phuean-ruam-chan)

Homework

การบ้าน

(Kan-ban)

Pen

ปากกา
(Pak-ka)

Pencil

ดินสอ

(Din-so)

Eraser

ยางลบ

(Yang-lop)

Paper

กระดาษ

(Kra-dat)

Notebook

สมุดบันทึก

(Sa-mut-ban-thuek)

Book

หนังสือ

(Nang-sue)

Folder

แฟ้ม

(Faem)

Backpack

กระเป๋าสะพาย

(Kra-pao-sa-phai)

Board

กระดาษ

(Kra-dat)

Chalk

ชอล์ก

(Chalk)

Hotels & Lodging – โรงแรมและที่พักชั่วคราว – Rong-raem-lae-thi-phak- Chua-khrao

Hotel

โรงแรม

(Rong-raem)

Guest

แขก

(*Khaek*)

Hostel

ที่พัก

(Thi-phak)

Youth hostel

บ้านพักเยาวชน

(Ban-phak-yao-wa-chon)

Room

ห้อง

(Hong)

Reservation

จอง

(Chong)

Check in

ลงทะเบียนเข้าพัก

(Long-tha-bian-khao-phak)

Bed

เตียง

(Tiang)

Boarding house

บ้านที่มีทั้งห้องพักและอาหาร

(Ban-thi-mi-thang –hong-phak-lae-a-han)

Double room

ห้องที่มีเตียงคู่

(Hong-thi-mi-tiang-khu)

Key

กุญแจ

(Kun-chae)

Do you have the keys?

คุณมีกุญแจไหม

(Khun-mi-kun-chae-mai)

Elevator

ลิฟท์

(Lift)

Double bed

เตียงคู่

(tiang-khu)

King-size bed

เตียงคู่

(tiang-khu)

Lobby

ห้องรับรอง

(Hong-rap-rong)

Room service

รูมเซอร์วิส

(Room service)

How much per night?

คืนละเท่าไร

(Khuen-la-thao-rai)

Is there anything cheaper?

มีถูกกว่านี้ไหม

(Mi-thuk-kwa-ni-mai)

Hi, I wanted to reserve a room for this weekend

สวัสดี ฉันอยากจะจองห้องพักสุดสัปดาห์ที่จะถึงนี้

(Sa-wat-di-chan-yak-cha-chong-hong-phak-sut-sap-da-thi-cha-thueng-ni)

For how many people?

สำหรับกี่คน

(Sam-rap-ki-khon)

Is there Wifi in the room?

ในห้องมีวายฟายไหม

(Nai-hong-mi-wai-fai-mai)

Concierge

คนเฝ้าประตู

(Khon-fao-pra-tu)

Five-star

ห้าดาว

(Ha-dao)

Gym

โรงยิม

(Rong-yim)

Pool

สระว่ายน้ำ

(Sa-wai-nam)

I have a reservation

ฉันมีจองไว้

(Chan-mi-chong-wai)

Rooftop terrace

ดาดฟ้า

(Dat-fa)

Beach

ชายหาด

(Chai-hat)

How far is the hotel from the beach?

โรงแรมไกลจากชายหาดขนาดไหน

(Rong-raem-kai-chak-chai-hat-kha-nat-nai)

Extra bed

เตียงเสริม

(Tiang-soem)

Bathtub

อ่างอาบน้ำ

(Ang-ap-nam)

Hairdryer

ที่เป่าผม

(Thi-pao-phom)

Hanger

ไม้แขวนเสื้อ

(Mai-khwaen-suea)

Sink

อ่างล้างมือ

(Ang-lang-mue)

Window

หน้าต่าง

(Na-tang)

Pillow

หมอน

(Mon)

Lamp

โคมไฟ

(Khom-fai)

Safe (lockbox)

ตู้นิรภัย

(Tu-ni-ra-phai)

Shower

ฝักบัว

(Fak-bua)

Shampoo

น้ำยาสระผม

(Namya-sa-phom)

Television

โทรทัศน์

(Tho-ra-that)

Toilet

ห้องน้ำ

(Hong-nam)

Sheets

ผ้าปูที่นอน

(*Pha-pu-thi-non*)

Towel

ผ้าเช็ดตัว

(Pha-chet-tua)

Water

น้ำ

(Nam)

I'll be staying three nights

ฉันขอพักสามคืน

(Chan-kho-phak-sam-khuen)

Please give me a wake-up call at 8 a.m.

ช่วยโทรปลุกฉันตอนแปดโมงเช้า

(Chuai-tho-pluk-chan-ton-paet-mong-chao)

Our room hasn't been cleaned

ห้องเรายังไม่ได้ทำความสะอาดเลย

(Hong-rao-yang-mai-dai-tham-khwam-sa-at-loeih)

Are there any rooms available?

มีห้องว่างไหม

(Mi-hong-wang-mai)

Sorry, we're full

ต้องขอโทษด้วย ห้องเราเต็มแล้ว

(Tong-kho-thot-duai-hong-rao-tem-laeo)

Suite

ห้องชุด

(Hong-chut)

Air conditioning

เครื่องปรับอากาศ

(Khrueang-prap-a-kat)

Check out is at 11:00 am

แจ้งออกตอนสิบเอ็ดโมงเช้า

(Chaeng-Ok-ton-sip-et-mong-chao)

Boarding house

บ้านที่มีทั้งห้องพักและอาหาร

(Ban-thi-mi-thang-hong-phak-lae-a-han)

Full board

มีอาหารให้เช้า กลางวัน เย็น

(Mi –a-han-hai-chao-klang-wan-yen)

Half board

มีอาหารให้ เช้า เย็น

(Mi –a-han-hai-chao-yen)

I would like…

ฉันอยากได้…

(Chan-yak-dai)

I'd like a room with a view

ฉันอยากได้ห้องที่มีทิวทัศน์

(Chan-yak-dai-hong-thi-mi-thio-that)

Balcony

ระเบียง

(Ra-biang)

I'd like a room with a balcony

ฉันอยากได้ห้องที่มีระเบียง

(Chan-yak-dai-hong –thi-mi-ra-biang)

Porter

เด็กยกกระเป๋า

(Dek-yok-kra-pao)

Bellhop

เด็กยกกระเป๋า

(Dek-yok-kra-pao)

Manager

ผู้จัดการ

(Phu-chat-kan)

I'd like to speak with the manager

ฉันอยากคุยกับผู้จัดการ

(Chan-yak-khui-kap-phu-chat-kan)

Bill

ใบเสร็จ

(Bai-set)

Receipt

ใบเสร็จ

(Bai-set)

Feelings – ความรู้สึก – Khwam-ru-suek

To be

เป็น

(Pen)

I am...

ฉันรู้สึก...

(Chan-ru-suek...)

Sad

เศร้า

(Sao)

Happy

มีความสุข

(Mi-khwam-suk)

Unhappy

ไม่มีความสุข

(Mai- mi-khwam-suk)

Angry

โกรธ

(Krot)

Confused

สับสน

(Sap-son)

In love

ตกหลุมรัก

(Tok-lum-rak)

Stressed

เครียด

(Khriat)

Overwhelmed

กดดัน

(Kot-dan)

Strong

แข็งแกร่ง

(Khaeng-kraeng)

Weak

อ่อนแอ

(On-ae)

Hurt

เจ็บ

(Chep)

Does it hurt?

เจ็บไหม

(Chep-mai)

Exciting

ตื่นเต้น

(Tuen-ten)

Boring

เบื่อ

(Buea)

Timid

อาย

(Ai)

Tired

เหนื่อย

(Nueai)

Frieghtened

กลัว

(Klua)

I am scared

ฉันกลัว

(Chan-klua)

Jealous

อิจฉา

(It-cha)

Surprised

แปลกใจ

(Plaek-chai)

Content

พอใจ

(Pho-chai)

Nervous

ประหม่า

(Pra-ma)

Busy

ยุ่ง

(Yung)

Worried

กังวล

(Kang-won)

Furious

โกรธมาก

(Krot-mak)

It's embarassing for me

มันน่าอายสำหรับฉัน

(Man-na-ai-sam-rap-chan)

Confident

มั่นใจ

(Man-chai)

Confidence

ความมั่นใจ

(Khwam-man-chai_

Sure

แน่ใจ

(Nae-chai)

Anxious

วิตกกังวล

(Wi-tok-kang-won)

Depressed

ซึมเศร้า

(Suem-sao)

Patient

อดทน

(Ot-thon)

Proud

ภูมิใจ

(Phum-chai)

Relieved

โล่งอก

(Long-ok)

Restless

ร้อนใจ

(Ron-chai)

Satisfied

พอใจ

(Pho-chai)

Sensitive

อ่อนไหว

(On-wai)

Uncomfortable

อึดอัด

(Uet-at)

Comfortable

สบาย

(Sa-bai)

Desperate

สิ้นหวัง

(Sin-wang)

Frustrated

หงุดหงิด

(Ngut-ngit)

Relaxed

ผ่อนคลาย

(Phon-khlai)

Insecure

ไม่ปลอดภัย

(Mai-plot-phai)

Delighted

ปลื้มปิติ

(Pluem-pi-ti)

Are you sure?

คุณแน่ใจใช่ไหม

(Khun-nae-chai-chai-mai)

I don't feel well

ฉันรู้สึกไม่ค่อยดี

(Chan-ru-suek-mai-khoi-di)

How are you feeling?

คุณรู้สึกเป็นยังไง

(Khun-ru-suek-pen-yang-ngai)

I'm fed up

ฉันเอือมระอา

(Chan-ueam-ra-a)

Sea sick, nausea

คลื่นไส้

(Khluen-sai)

I'm ill

ฉันป่วย

(Chan-puai)

I don't feel like going out

ฉันไม่อยากออกจากบ้าน

(Chan-mai-yak-ok-chak-ban)

Fancy, feel like

รู้สึกอยากที่จะ

(Ru-suek-yak-thi-cha)

Eating, Drinking, & Nightlife – กิน ดื่ม เที่ยวกลางคืน – Kin-duem-thiao-klang-khuen

Eat out

กินข้าวนอกบ้าน

(Kin-khao-nok-ban)

Restaurant

ร้านอาหาร

(Ran-a-han)

Fast food

อาหารจานด่วน

(A-han-chan-duan)

Gastronomy

การกินอาหารดี

(Kan-kin-a-han-di)

Breakfast

อาหารเช้า

(A-han-chao)

Lunch

อาหารกลางวัน

(A-han-klang-wan)

Dinner

อาหารเย็น

(A-han-yen)

Where is a good restaurant?

แถวนี้มีร้านอาหารดีๆที่ไหนบ้าง

(Thaeo-ni-mi-ran-a-han-di-di-thi-nai-bang)

Do you know a good place to eat?

คุณมีร้านอาหารดีๆแนะนำไหม

(Khun-mi-ran-a-han-di-di-nae-nam-mai)

I would like to make a reservation

ฉันต้องการจะจองที่นั่ง

(Chan-tong-kan-cha-chong-thi-nang)

Table for two

โต๊ะสำหรับสองคน

(To-sam-rap-song-khon)

Menu

เมนู

(Menu)

Appetizers

อาหารเรียกน้ำย่อย

(A-han-riak-nam-yoi)

Main course

อาหารจานหลัก

(A-han-chan-lak)

Dessert

ของหวาน

(Khong-wan)

What would you like to drink?

คุณอยากจะดื่มอะไร

(*Khun-yak-cha-duem-a-rai*)

A glass of water, please

ขอน้ำเปล่าหนึ่งแก้ว

(Kho-nam-plao-nueng-kaeo)

coffee with milk, latte

กาแฟใส่นม,ลาเต้

(Ka-fae-sai-nom , La-t)e

Beer

เบียร์

(Beer)

Wine

ไวน์

(Wine)

Red wine

ไวน์แดง

(Wine-daeng)

White wine

ไวน์ขาว

(Wine-khao)

Whisky

วิสกี้

(Whisky)

Vodka

วอดก้า

(Vodka)

Rum

เหล้ารัม

(Lao-rum)

Gin

เหล้ายิน

(Lao-yin)

Craft beer

คราฟท์เบียร์

(Craft-beer)

Vegetarian

มังสวิรัติ

(Mang-sa-wi-rat)

Check, please

เก็บตัง

(Kep-tang)

Tip

ติป

(Tip)

Cheers!

ชนแก้ว

(Chon-kaeo)

It's delicious!

มันอร่อยมาก

(Man-a-roi-mak)

Enjoy your meal

ทานให้อร่อย

(Than-hai-a-roi)

Plate

จาน

(Charn)

To be hungry

หิว

(Hio)

I'm hungry

ฉันหิว

(Chan-hio)

Eat healthy

กินเพื่อสุขภาพ

(Kin-phuea-suk-kha-phap)

Fork

ส้อม

(Som)

Knife

มีด

(Meet)

Spoon

ช้อน

(Chon)

Napkin

ผ้าเช็ดปาก

(Pha-chet-pak)

Glass

แก้ว

(Kaeo)

Bottle

ขวด

(Khuat)

Ice

น้ำแข็ง

(Nam-khaeng)

Salt

เกลือ

(Kluea)

Pepper

พริกไทย

(Phrik-thai)

Sugar

น้ำตาล

(Nam-tan)

Soup

น้ำแกง

(Nam-kaeng)

Salad

สลัด

(Salad)

Bread

ขนมปัง

(Kha-nom-pang)

Butter

เนย

(Noei)

Noodles

บะหมี่

(Ba-mi)

Rice

ข้าว

(Khao)

Cheese

ชีส

(Cheese)

Vegetables

ผัก

(Phak)

Asparagus

หน่อไม้ฝรั่ง

(No-mai-fa-rang)

Beans

ถั่ว

(Thua)

Beet

หัวบีท

(Hua-beet)

Broccoli

บรอคโคลี่

(*Broccoli*)

Carrot

แครอท

(Carrot)

Artichoke

อาร์ติโชค

(Artichoke)

Cabbage

กะหล่ำปลี

(Ka-lam-pli)

Cauliflower

กะหล่ำดอก

(Ka-lam-dok)

Tomato

มะเขือเทศ

(Ma-khuea-thet)

Chickpea

ถั่วลูกไก่

(Thua-luk-kai)

Corn

ข้าวโพด

(Khao-phot)

Cucumber

แตงกวา

(Taeng-kwa)

Potato

มันฝรั่ง

(Man-fa-rang)

Sweet potato

มันเทศ

(Man-thet)

Mushroom

เห็ด

(Het)

Pepper

พริก

(Phrik)

Onion

หอมหัวใหญ่

(Hom-hua-yai)

Spinach

ผักโขม

(Phak-khom)

Chicken

ไก่

(kai)

Beef

เนื้อวัว

(Nuea-wua)

Pork

เนื้อหมู

(Nuea-mu)

Fish

ปลา

(pla)

Spicy

เผ็ด

(phet)

Sweet

หวาน

(wan)

Sour

เปรี้ยว

(Priao)

Ice cream

ไอศกรีม

(Ai-sa-krim)

Juice

น้ำผลไม้

(Nam-phon-la-mai)

Pie/Cake

พาย/เค้ก

(pie/cake)

Fruit

ผลไม้

(phon-la-mai)

Apple

แอปเปิ้ล

(Apple)

Plantain

กล้วยกล้าย

(*Kluai-klai*)

Banana

กล้วย

(kluai)

Peach

ลูกพีช

(Luk-peach)

Blueberry

ผลบลูเบอร์รี่

(Phon-blueberry)

Cherry
เชอร์รี่

(Cherry)

Grape
องุ่น

(A-ngun)

Lemon
มะนาวเหลือง

(Ma-nao-lueang)

Lime
มะนาวเขียว

(Ma-nao-khiao)

Pineapple
สับปะรด

(Sap-pa-rot)

Orange

ส้ม

(Som)

Watermelon

แตงโม

(Taeng-mo)

Raspberry

ราสเบอร์รี่

(Raspberry)

Strawberry

สตรอว์เบอร์รี่

(Strawberry)

Pear

ลูกแพร์

(Luk-pear)

Avocado

อาโวคาโด

(Avocado)

Alcohol

แอลกอฮอล์

(Alcohol)

Drink (alcoholic)

สุรา

(Su-ra)

Cocktail

ค็อกเทล

(Cocktail)

Pub

ผับ

(Pub)

Tavern

โรงเหล้า

(Rong-lao)

Bar

บาร์

(Bar)

Concert

คอนเสิร์ต

(Concert)

Nightclub

ไนต์คลับ

(Nightclub)

Dance

เต้น

(Ten)

Let's go have a drink

ไปหาอะไรดื่มกัน

(Pai-ha-a-rai-duem-kan)

Go out

ไปข้างนอก

(Pai-khang-nok)

Go out to party

ไปงานกินเลี้ยง

(Pai-ngan-kin-liang)

Party

กินเลี้ยง

(kin-liang)

Bar hop

ดื่มหลายที่

(Duem-lai-thi)

To go bar hopping

ไปดื่มหลายที่

(Pai-duem-lai-thi)

Do I need a reservation?

ฉันต้องจองไหม

(Chan-tong-chong-mai)

Can I see the menu please?

ฉันขอดูเมนูหน่อย

(Chan-kho-du-menu-noi)

What do you recommend?

คุณมีอะไรแนะนำไหม

(*Khun-mi-a-rai-nae-nam-mai*)

I'm a vegetarian

ฉันเป็นมังสวิรัติ

(Chan-pen-mang-sa-wi-rat)

I'm a vegan

ฉันเป็นมังสวิรัติ

(Chan-pen-mang-sa-wi-rat)

I can't have...

ฉันกิน ... ไม่ได้

(Chan-kin ... mai-dai)

I'm allergic to...

ฉันแพ้ ...

(Chan-phae ...)

I'm allergic to nuts/ seafood

ฉันแพ้ถั่ว / อาหารทะเล

(Chan-phae-thua / A-han-tha-le)

I'm lactose intolerant

ฉันเป็นภาวะการย่อยกรดแลคโตสผิดปกติ

(Chan-pen-pha-wa-kan-yoi-krot-lactose-phit-pok-ka-ti)

What are today's specials?

วันนี้มีเมนูพิเศษอะไร

(Wan-ni-mi-menu-phi-set-a-rai)

I'd like to try a regional dish

ฉันอยากลองกินอาหารพื้นเมือง

(Chan-yak-long-kin-a-han-phuen-mueang)

Can you bring me the check, please?

ช่วยเอาเช็คมาให้ผมหน่อยได้ไหม

(Chuai-ao-chek-ma-hai-phom-noi-dai-mai)

I'm on a diet

ฉันกำลังลดน้ำหนัก

(Chan-kam-lang-lot-nam-nak)

What is in it?

นี่ทำมาจากอะไร

(Ni-tham-ma-chak-a-rai)

Hobbies & Sports – งานอดิเรกและกีฬา – Ngan-a-di-rek-lae-ki-la

What are your hobbies?

คุณมีงานอดิเรกอะไร

(*Khun-mi-ngan-a-di-rek-a-rai*)

Free time

เวลาว่าง

(We-la-wang)

I am a fan of...

ฉันชอบ...มาก

(Chan-chop ... mak)

I like...

ฉันชอบ...

(Chan-chop)

To sing

ร้องเพลง

(Rong-phleng)

To play sports

เล่นกีฬา

(Len-kila)

To listen to music

ฟังเพลง

(Fang-phleng)

To ride a bike

ขี่จักรยาน

(Khi-chak-kra-yan)

To fish

ตกปลา

(Tok-pla)

To swim

ว่ายน้ำ

(Wai-nam)

To collect stamps

สะสมแสตมป์

(Sa-som-sa-taem)

To play music

เล่นดนตรี

(Len-don-tri)

To play an instrument

เล่นเครื่องดนตรี

(Len-khrueang-don-tri)

Guitar

กีตาร์

(Guitar)

Drums

กลอง

(Klong)

Piano

เปียโน

(Piano)

Trumpet

แตร

(Trae)

To hunt

ล่า

(Lar)

To work out

ออกกำลังกาย

(Ok-kam-lang-kai)

To run

วิ่ง

(Wing)

To cook

ทำอาหาร

(Tham-a-han)

To sew

เย็บผ้า

(Yep-pha)

Hiking

เดินทางไกล

(Doen-thang-kai)

Photography

ถ่ายรูป

(Thai-rup)

Sailing

ล่องเรือ

(Long-ruea)

Chess

หมากรุก

(Mak-ruk)

Stadium

สนามกีฬา

(Sa-nam-ki-la)

Court

สนาม

(Sa-nam)

Pitch (Soccer)

สนามบอล

(Sa-nam-ball)

Field

สนาม

(Sa-nam)

Baseball

เบสบอล

(Baseball)

Basketball

บาสเกตบอล

(Basketball)

Football

อเมริกันฟุตบอล

(American Football)

Soccer

ฟุตบอล

(*Football*)

Golf

กอล์ฟ

(Golf)

Hockey

ฮอคกี้

(Hockey)

Boxing

ชกมวย

(Chok-muai)

Tennis

เทนนิส

(Tennis)

Volleyball

วอลเล่ย์บอล

(Volleyball)

To ski

เล่นสกี

(Len-ski)

Snowboard

สโนว์บอร์ด

(Snowboard)

Mountain climb

ปีนเขา

(Pin-khao)

To go surfing

เล่นโต้คลื่น

(Len-to-khluen)

To travel

ท่องเที่ยว

(Thong-thiao)

To go on vacation

หยุดงานไปเที่ยวพักผ่อน

(Yut-ngan-pai-thiao-phak-phon)

Watch a game

ดูเกมการแข่งขัน

(Du-kem-kan-khaeng-khan)

Sports game

เกมกีฬา

(Kem-ki-la)

To read

อ่าน

(An)

Read books

อ่านหนังสือ

(An-nang-sue)

To paint

ระบายสี

(Ra-bai-si)

To draw

วาดรูป

(Wat-rup)

Gardening

จัดสวน

(Chat-suan)

Go to the cinema

ไปดูหนัง

(Pai-du-nang)

Common Questions & Answers – คำถามและคำตอบทั่วๆไป – Kham-tham lae-kham-top-thua-thua-pai

Who is it?

ใครนะ

(Khrai-na)

What is your surname?

นามสกุลของคุณคือ

(Nam-sa-kun-khong-khun-khue)

Where did you come from?

คุณมาจากไหน

(Khun-ma-chak-nai)

Where were you born?

คุณเกิดที่ไหน

(*Khun-koet-thi-nai*)

I was born in...

ฉันเกิดที่...

(Chan-koet-thi)

How old are you?

คุณอายุเท่าไร

(*Khun-ayu-thao-rai*)

I am thirty years old

ฉันอายุสามสิบ

(Chan-ayu-sam-sip)

Do you have any siblings?

คุณมีพี่น้องไหม

(Khun-mi-phi-nong-mai)

What is your phone number?

เบอร์โทรคุณเบอร์อะไร

(Boe-tho-khun-boe-a-rai)

What is the date today?

วันนี้วันที่เท่าไร

(Wan-ni-wan-thi-thao-rai)

Do you have pets?

คุณมีสัตว์เลี้ยงไหม

(Khun-mi-sat-liang-mai)

What is the weather like?

อากาศเป็นยังไง

(*A-kat-pen-yang-ngai*)

It's sunny

แดดจ้า

(Dad-ja)

It's raining

ฝนตก

(Fon-tok)

It's snowing

หิมะตก

(Hi-ma-tok)

It's nice out

ข้างนอกอากาศดี

(Khang-nok-a-kat-di)

It's humid

อากาศชื้น

(A-kat-chuen)

It's cloudy

เมฆครึ้ม

(Mek-khruem)

There's lightning

มีฟ้าผ่า

(Mi-fa-pha)

There's thunder

มีฟ้าร้อง

(Mi-fa-rong)

How much?

เท่าไร

(*Thao-rai*)

How much is it?

อันนี้เท่าไร

(*An-ni-thao-rai*)

How much does it cost?

ราคาเท่าไร

(*Ra-kha-thao-rai*)

What do you want?

คุณอยากได้อะไร

(*Khun-yak-dai-a-rai*)

What do you want to do?

คุณอยากทำอะไร

(*Khun-yak-tham-a-rai*)

Is it hot? (weather)

อากาศร้อนไหม

(A-kat-ron-mai)

Yes, it is hot (weather)

ใช่ อากาศร้อน

(Chai-a-kat-ron)

Is it cold? (weather)

อาการหนาวไหม

(A-kan-nao-mai)

Yes, it is cold (weather)

ใช่ อากาศหนาว

(*Chai-a-kat-nao*)

Is it hot? (object)

มันร้อนไหม

(Man-ron-mai)

Yes, it is hot (object)

ใช่ มันร้อน

(Chai- man-ron)

Is it cold? (object)

มันเย็นไหม

(Man-yen-mai)

Yes, it is cold (object)

ใช่ มันเย็น

(Chai-man-yen)

How many are there?

มันมีกี่ชิ้น

(*Man-mi-ki-chin*)

Can you repeat that, please?

ช่วยพูดอีกรอบได้ไหม

(Chuai-phut-ik-rop-dai-mai)

What is that?

นั่นคืออะไร

(*Nan-khue-a-rai*)

Do you understand?

คุณเข้าใจไหม

(Khun-khao-chai-mai)

Do you speak English?

คุณพูดอังกฤษได้ไหม

(Khun-phut-ang-krit-dai-mai)

Yes, I speak English

ได้ ฉันพูดอังกฤษได้

(*Dai-chan-phut-ang-krit-dai*)

Where are you going?

คุณจะไปที่ไหน

(Khun-cha-pai-thi-nai)

I'm going over there

ฉันจะไปตรงนั้น

(Chan-cha-pai-trong-nan)

Where is it?

มันอยู่ที่ไหน

(*Man-yu-thi-nai*)

It's over there

มันอยู่ตรงนั้น

(Man-yu-trong-nan)

Why not?

ทำไมจะไม่ละ

(Tham-mai-cha-mai-la)

Why is that?

ทำไมล่ะ

(Tham-mai-la)

Whose is that?

นั่นของใคร

(Nan-khong-khrai)

It's his

มันเป็นของเขา

(Man-pen-khong-khao)

What color is this?

นี่สีอะไร

(*Ni-si-a-rai*)

What is your favorite color?

สีโปรดคุณคือสีอะไร

(*Si-prot-khun-khue-si-a-rai*)

Can you help me, please?

คุณช่วยฉันหน่อยได้ไหม

(Khun-chuai-chan-noi-dai-mai)

Where is the bathroom?

ห้องน้ำอยู่ไหน

(*Hong-nam-yu-nai*)

Is there an ATM around here?

แถวนี้มีตู้เอทีเอ็มไหม

(Thaeo-ni-mi-tu-ATM-mai)

Why? For what purpose?

ทำไปเพื่อจุดประสงค์อะไร

(Tham-pai-phuea-chut-pra-song-a-rai)

Of what? From what?

ของอะไร จากอะไร

(Khong-a-rai-chak-a-rai)

Who should I contact?

ฉันควรติดต่อใคร

(Chan-khuan-tit-to-khrai)

How do you spell your name?

ชื่อคุณสะกดยังไง

(*Chue-khun-sa-kot-yang-ngai*)

Any questions?

มีคำถามอะไรไหม

(Mi-kham-tham-a-rai-mai)

Which?

อันไหน

(*An-nai*)

Who is he/she?

เขา/เธอ คือใคร

(Khao-tap-thoe-khue-khrai)

When did you arrive?

คุณมาถึงเมื่อไร

(*Khun-ma-thueng-muea-rai*)

I arrived last night

ฉันมาถึงเมื่อคืน

(*Chan-ma-thueng-muea-khuen*)

Which is better?

อันไหนดีกว่ากัน

(*An-nai-di-kwa-kan*)

This is better

อันนี้ดีกว่า

(*An-ni-di-kwa*)

How?

ยังไง

(*Yang-ngai*)

Where did they go?

พวกเขาไปไหน

(Phuak-khao-pai-nai)

Is he/she here?

เขา/เธอ อยู่ที่นี่ไหม

(*Khao/thoe-yu-thi-ni-mai*)

No, he/she left

ไม่ เขา/เธอ ไปแล้ว

(Mai-khao/thoe-pai-laeo)

How many?

เท่าไร

(*Thao-rai*)

Why?

ทำไม

(Tham-mai)

Because...

เพราะ...

(Phro)

How did you do that?

คุณทำแบบนั้นได้ยังไง

(*Khun-tham-baep-nan-dai-yang-ngai*)

Of course

แน่นอน

(Nae-non)

Of course

แน่นอน

(Nae-non)

What time do you open?

ร้านคุณเปิดกี่โมง

(Ran-khun-poet-ki-mong)

What time do you close?

ร้านคุณปิดกี่โมง

(Ran-khun-pit-ki-mong)

How much do I owe you?

ฉันติดคุณเท่าไร

(*Chan-tit-khun-thao-rai*)

Can I pay with card?

ใช้บัตรเครดิตได้ไหม

(Chai-bat-khre-dit-dai-mai)

Can you deliver it to my hotel?

ช่วยส่งไปที่โรงแรมของฉันได้ไหม

(Chuai-song-pai-thi-rong-raem-khong-chan-dai-mai)

Reacting to Good News – การตอบสนองต่อข่าวดี – Kan-top-sa-nong-to- khao-di

Very well
ดีมาก

(Di-mak)

How nice
ดีจริงๆ

(*Di-ching-ching*)

I'm pleased
ฉันพอใจ

(Chan-pho-chai)

I appreciate it
ฉันเห็นค่ามัน

(Chan-hen-kha-man)

Congratulations! (accomplishments)

ยินดีด้วย

(Yin-di-duai)

Congratulations! (birthdays, anniversaries, celebrations)

ยินดีด้วย

(Yin-di-duai)

Happy birthday

สุขสันต์วันเกิด

(Suk-san-wan-koet)

Very well

ดีมาก

(Di-mak)

It is very good (useful)

มันดีมาก

(Man-di-mak)

Really?

จริงหรอ

(Ching-ro)

Count me in

ฉันร่วมด้วย

(Chan-ruam-duai)

I'm all for it

ฉันสนับสนุนเต็มที่

(Chan-sa-nap-sa-nun-tem-thi)

Perfect

สมบูรณ์แบบ

(Som-bu-baep)

Stupendous

มโหฬาร

(Ma-ho-lan)

Marvelous

น่าพิศวง

(Na-phit-sa-wong)

Absolutely

แน่นอน

(Nae-non)

Awesome

ยอดเยี่ยม

(Yot-yiam)

That's it

เท่านี้แหละ

(Thao-ni-lae)

That's why

นั่นคือเหตุผล

(Nan-khue-het-phon)

Good job

ทำได้ดี

(Tham-dai-di)

Magnificent

เลิศ

(Loet)

That's how you do it

นั่นคือวิธีทำ

(Nan-khue-wi-thi-tham)

Brilliant

หลักแหลม

(Lak-laem)

Genius

อัจฉริยะ

(At-cha-ri-ya)

Good idea

ความคิดดี

(Khwam-khit-di)

Excellent

เยี่ยม

(Yiam)

Incredible

เหลือเชื่อ

(Luca-chuca)

Why not?

ทำไมไม่ละ

(Tham-mai-mai-la)

Ok

โอเค

(Okay)

Phenomenal

มหัศจรรย์

(Ma-hat-sa-chan)

Funny

ตลก

(Ta-lok)

Fun

สนุก

(Sa-nuk)

I had a good time

ฉันมีช่วงเวลาที่ดี

(Chan-mi-chuang-we-la-thi-di)

What are you doing? — คุณกำลังทำอะไร — Khun-kam-lang-tham-a-rai

What are you doing later?

หลังจากนี้คุณจะทำอะไร

(*Lang-chak-ni-khun-cha-tham-a-rai*)

What's your plan?

คุณมีแผนอะไร

(*Khun-mi-phaen-a-rai*)

Do you have plans?

คุณมีแผนอะไรไหม

(*Khun-mi-phaen-a-rai-mai*)

Do you have planes tonight?

คืนนี้มีเครื่องบินไหม

(*Khuen-ni-mi-khrueang-bin-mai*)

Are you going out tonight?

คืนนี้ไปข้างนอกหรือเปล่า

(Khuen-ni-pai-khang-nok-rue-plao)

Clothing & Appearance – เครื่องแต่งกายและรูปลักษณ์ภายนอก - Khrueang-taeng-kai-lae-rup-lak-phai-nok

Handsome (men)

หล่อ

(Lo)

Pretty (woman)

สวย

(Suai)

Pretty

น่ารัก

(Na-rak)

Beautiful

สวยงาม

(Suai-ngam)

Young

เด็ก

(Dek)

Old

แก่

(Kae)

Ugly

น่าเกลียด

(Na-kliat)

Good looking

ดูดี

(Du-di)

Smooth

เนียน

(Nian)

T-shirt
เสื้อทีเชิ้ต

(Suea-thi-choet)

Shirt
เสื้อเชิ้ต

(Suea-choet)

Blouse
เสื้อสตรี

(Suea-sa-thi)

Dress
กระโปรงชุด

(Kra-prong-chut)

Bra
ยกทรง
(Yok-song)

Knickers/Panties

กางเกงใน

(Kang-keng-nai)

Tights

ถุงน่อง

(Thung-nong)

To dress

แต่งตัว

(Taeng-tua)

Shoes

รองเท้า

(Rong-thao)

High heels

รองเท้าส้นสูง

(Rong-thao-son-sung)

Sneakers/Trainers

รองเท้าผ้าใบ

(Rong-thao-pha-bai)

Pants/trousers

กางเกงขายาว

(Kang-keng-kha-yao)

Jeans

กางเกงยีนส์

(Kang-keng-yin)

Socks

ถุงเท้า

(Thung-thao)

Underwear

ชุดชั้นใน

(Chut-chan-nai)

Shorts

กางเกงขาสั้น

(Kang-keng-kha-san)

Suit

ชุดสูท

(Chut-sut)

Tie

เนคไท

(Nek-thai)

Scarf

ผ้าพันคอ

(Pha-phan-kho)

Ring

แหวน

(Waen)

Jewelry

เครื่องเพชร

(Khrueang-phet)

Hat

หมวก

(Muak)

Glasses

แว่น

(Waen)

Sunglasses

แว่นกันแดด

(Waen-kan-daet)

Sleeves

แขนเสื้อ

(Khaen-suea)

Size

ไซส์

(Size)

To dress nice

แต่งตัวดี

(Taeng-tua-di)

Belt

เข็มขัด

(Khem-khat)

Button

กระดุม

(Kra-dum)

Bracelet

กำไลข้อมือ

(Kam-lai-kho-mue)

Watch

นาฬิกาข้อมือ

(Na-li-ka-kho-mue)

Necklace

สร้อยคอ

(Soi-kho)

Earrings

ต่างหู

(Tang-hu)

Dress code

ข้อบังคับการแต่งตัว

(*Kho-bang-khap-kan-taeng-tua*)

Dry cleaner's

ร้านซักแห้ง

(Ran-sak-haeng)

Stain

รอยเปื้อน

(Roi-puean)

Detergent

ผงซักฟอก

(Phong-sak-fok)

To iron

รีด

(Rit)

Short

สั้น

(San)

Long

ยาว

(Yao)

Straight (hair)

ผมตรง

(Phom-trong)

Curly

ผมหยิก

(Phom-yik)

Blond

ผมบลอนด์

(Phom-blon)

Red-head

ผมสีแดง

(Phom-si-daeng)

Light brown

น้ำตาลอ่อน

(Nam-tan-on)

Dark brown

น้ำตาลเข้ม

(Nam-tan-khem)

Black

ดำ

(Dam)

Gray

เทา

(Thao)

Tall

สูง

(Sung)

Short

เตี้ย

(Tia)

Medium

ปานกลาง

(Pan-klang)

Fat

อ้วน

(Uan)

Thin

ผอม

(Phom)

Red

แดง

(Daeng)

Blue

น้ำเงิน

(Nam-ngoen)

Green

เขียว

(Khiao)

Light

อ่อน

(On)

Dark

เข้ม

(Khem)

What do you look like?

ลักษณะคุณเป็นยังไง

(*Lak-sa-na-khun-pen-yang-ngai*)

Problem Solving – จัดการปัญหา – Chat-kan-pan-ha

Problem

ปัญหา

(Pan-ha)

To solve

แก้ปัญหา

(Kae-pan-ha)

Solution

ทางออก

(Thang-ok)

Mess

ความยุ่งเหยิง

(*Khwam-yung-yoeng*)

Big problem

ปัญหาใหญ่

(Pan-ha-yai)

Let's try this

ลองวิธีนี้ดู

(Long-wi-thi-ni-du)

To try

ลอง

(Long)

Intend

ตั้งใจ

(Tang-chai)

Issue

ปัญหา

(Pan-ha)

Matter

ปัญหา

(Pan-ha)

Solve the matter

แก้ปัญหา

(Kae- Pan-ha)

What's the problem?

มีปัญหาอะไร

(*Mi-pan-ha-a-rai*)

What's the matter with you?

คุณมีปัญหาอะไร

(*Khun-mi-pan-ha-a-rai*)

Don't get annoyed

ไม่รู้สึกรำคาญ

(Mai-ru-suek-ram-khan)

Cheer up

ร่าเริงหน่อย

(*Ra-roeng-noi*)

The Body – ร่างกาย

Head

หัว

(Hua)

Neck

คอ

(Kho)

Shoulders

ไหล่

(Lai)

Chest

อก

(Ok)

Arms

แขน

(Khaen)

Waist

เอว

(Eo)

Hips

สะโพก

(Sa-pok)

Wrist

ข้อมือ

(Kho-mue)

Hands

มือ

(Mue)

Fingers

นิ้ว

(Nio)

Nails

เล็บ

(Lep)

Legs

ขา

(Kha)

Ankle

ข้อเท้า

(Kho-thao)

Heel

ส้นเท้า

(Son-thao)

Feet

เท้า

(Thao)

Toes

นิ้วเท้า

(Nio- Thao)

Knee

เข่า

(Khao)

Elbow

ข้อศอก

(Kho-sok)

Buttocks

ก้น

(Kon)

Hair

ผม

(Phom)

Eyes

ตา

(Ta)

Nose

จมูก

(Cha-muk)

Ear

หู

(Hu)

Lips

ริมฝีปาก

(Rim-fi-pak)

Cheek

แก้ม

(Kaem)

Mustache

หนวด

(Nuat)

You're growing a mustache

คุณมีหนวดขึ้น

(Khun-mi-nuat-khuen)

Beard

เครา

(Khrao)

To shave

โกน

(Kon)

To wax

แว๊ก

(wax)

Bikini line

บิกินี่ไลน์

(Bikini line)

Underarms

รักแร้

(Rak-rae)

Bone

กระดูก

(Kra-duk)

Joint

ข้อต่อ

(Kho-to)

Break

หัก

(Hak)

Break a bone

กระดูกหัก

(Kra-duk-hak)

Have a headache

ปวดหัว

(Puat-hua

Toothache

ปวดฟัน

(Puat-fan)

Pull a muscle

กล้ามเนื้อยืดออก

(Klam-nuea-yuet-ok)

Haircut

ตัดผม

(Tat-phom)

Style your hair

จัดทรงผมของคุณ

(Chat-song-phom-khong-khun)

Airplanes & Airports – เครื่องบินและสนามบิน – Khrueang-bin-lae-sa-nam-bin

How long does it take to get to the airport?

ต้องใช้เวลาเท่าไรเดินทางไปสนามบิน

(Tong-chai-we-la-thao-rai-doen-thang-pai-sa-nam-bin)

Gate

ประตู

(Pra-tu)

Flight

เที่ยวบิน

(Thiao-bin)

Passengers

ผู้โดยสาร

(Phu-doi-san)

Luggage

กระเป๋าเดินทาง

(Kra-pao-doen-thang)

Bags

กระเป๋า

(Kra-pao)

Ticket

ตั๋ว

(Tua)

Boarding pass

บัตรผ่านขึ้นเครื่อง

(Bat-phan-khuen-khrueang)

Pilot

นักบิน

(Nak-bin)

Emergency exit

ทางออกฉุกเฉิน

(Thang-ok-chuk-choen)

Seat

ที่นั่ง

(Thi-nang)

Row

แถว

(Thaeo)

Flight attendant

พนักงานต้อนรับบนเครื่องบิน

(Pha-nak-ngan- ton-rap-bon-khrueang-bin)

Carry-on luggage

กระเป๋าที่เอาขึ้นเครื่องได้

(Kra-pao-thi-ao-khuen-khrueang-dai)

Arrival

เวลาถึง

(We-la-thueng)

What time do you arrive?

ถึงกี่โมง

(Thueng-ki-mong)

I arrive at 9:30 p.m.

ฉันมาถึงตอนสามทุ่มครึ่ง

(Chan-ma-thueng-ton-sam-thum-khrueng)

Departure

เวลาออก

(We-la-ok)

Take-off

เครื่องขึ้น

(Khrueang-khuen)

Landing

ลงจอด

(Long-chot)

Delay

การล่าช้า

(Kan-la-cha)

Why has the plane been delayed?

ทำไมเครื่องบินถึงออกช้ากว่ากำหนด

(Tham-mai-khrueang-bin-thueng-ok-cha-kwa-kam-not)

My seatbelt won't fasten

ฉันคาดเข็มขัดไม่ได้

(Chan-khat-khem-khat-mai-dai)

May I have a blanket?

ฉันขอผ้าห่มได้ไหม

(Chan-kho-pha-hom-dai-mai)

I'd like a vegetarian meal

ฉันขออาหารมังสวิรัติ

(chan-kho-a-han-mang-sa-wi-rat)

What time are we going to land?

เครื่องจะลงจอดกี่โมง

(Khrueang-cha-long-chot-ki-mong)

Can I change my seat?

ฉันขอเปลี่ยนที่นั่งได้ไหม

(Chan-kho-plian-thi-nang-dai-mai)

I'd like an aisle seat

ฉันอยากได้ที่นั่งติดทางเดิน

(Chan-yak-dai-thi-nang-tit-thang-doen)

I'd like a window seat

ฉันอยากได้ที่นั่งติดหน้าต่าง

(Chan-yak-dai-thi-nang-tit-na-tang)

What is the in-flight movie?

บนเครื่องมีหนังอะไรฉาย

(Bon-khrueang-mi-nang-a-rai-chai)

May I have some water?

ฉันขอน้ำหน่อยได้ไหม

(Chan-kho-nam-noi-dai-mai)

Sentence Starters – การเริ่มประโยค – Khan-roem-pra-yok

Do you have a sec?
มีเวลาสักแปปไหม
(Mi-we-la-sak-paep-mai)

Wow!
ว้าว
(Wow)

Damn!
โอ้โห
(O-ho)

Well, so what?
เออ แล้วไง
(Oe-laeo-ngai)

Well then…
ถ้าอย่างนั้นก็...
(Tha-yang-nan-ko …)

And you know what else?
นอกจากนั้นแล้วยังมีอะไรอีกรู้ไหม
(Nokchaknan-laeo-yang-mi-a-rai-ik-ru-mai)

On second thought, (I do want a beer!)
คิดดูอีกทีแล้ว (ได้เบียร์สักแก้วก็ดี)
(Khit-du-ik-thi-laeo (Dai-beer-sak-kaeo-ko-di))

What a relief!
โล่งอกจริงๆ
(*Long-ok-ching-ching*)

Well...
ถ้างั้น...

(Tha-ngan ...)

You'd better do it, because otherwise...
คุณควรจะทำมัน เพราะถ้าไม่อย่างงั้น...

(Khun-khuan-cha-tham-man-phro-tha-mai-yang-ngan ...)

I'd love to help you but...
ฉันอยากจะช่วยคุณนะแต่....

(Chan-yak-cha-chuai-khun-na-tae...)

Oops!
อุ๊บซ์

(Oops)

Let's see...
ไหนดูซิ

(Nai-du-si)

Ok, but...
ก็ได้นะแต่...

(Kodai-na-tae)

Trust me

เชื่อฉัน

(Chuea-chan)

Come on!

เร็วเข้า

(Reo-khao)

Maybe so, but…

ก็อาจจะใช่นะแต่

(Ko-at-cha-chai-na-tae)

Hey!

เห้ย

(Hey)

Look out

ระวัง

(Ra-wang)

On the contrary…

ในทางกลับกัน

(Nai-thang-klap-kan)

You don't say

จริงหรอ

(Ching-ro)

Excuse me...

ขอโทษนะ...

(Kho-thot-na)

Sorry, but...

ขอโทษนะแต่...

(Kho-thot-na-tae)

Do you know of a restaurant around here?

แถวนี้มีร้านอาหารบ้างไหม

(Thaeo-ni-mi-ran-a-han-bang-mai)

Shopping & Negotiating – การซื้อของและการต่อรอง – Kan-sue-khong-lae- kan-to-rong

Where are the shops?
ร้านขายของอยู่ตรงไหน

(Ran-khai-hong-yu-trong-nai)

I don't need any help, I'm just browsing, thanks
ยังไม่ต้องช่วยครับ ขอดูก่อน

(Yang-mai-tong-chuai-khrap-kho-du-kon)

Is this on sale?
อันนี้ลดราคาหรือเปล่า

(An-ni-lot-ra-kha-rue-plao)

I'm looking for a pair of jeans
ฉันกำลังอยากได้กางเกงยีนส์

(Chan-kam-lang-yak-dai-kang-keng-yin)

Do you have these jeans in a size 40?
มีกางเกงยีนส์ตัวนี้ไซส์สี่สิบไหม

(Mi-kang-keng-yin-tua-ni-sai-si-sip-mai)

Do you have them in stock?
มีของในสต๊อกไหม

(Mi-khong-nai-sa-tok-mai)

Where are the fitting rooms?

ห้องลองชุดอยู่ตรงไหน

(Hong-long-chut-yu-trong-nai)

Try it on

ลองใส่ดู

(Long-sai-do)

Where is the till?

จ่ายเงินตรงไหน

(Chai-ngoen-trong-nai)

How much is it?

ราคาเท่าไร

(Ra-kha-thao-rai)

Is this returnable?

ซื้อแล้วคืนได้ไหม

(Sue-laeo-khuen-dai-mai)

This item is damaged, can I get a discount?

ของอันนี้มีตำหนิ ลดราคาให้ฉันได้ไหม

(Khong-an-ni-mi-tam-ni-lot-ra-kha-hai-chan-dai-mai)

Do you do student discount?

มีลดราคาให้นักเรียนไหม

(Mi-lot-ra-kha-hai-nak-rian-mai)

Do you take card?

รับบัตรเครดิตไหม

(Rap-bat-khre-dit-mai)

Keep the change

ไม่ต้องทอน

(Mai-tong-thon)

May I have the receipt?

ขอใบเสร็จด้วยได้ไหม

(Kho-bai-set-duai-dai-mai)

You've charged me twice for this

คุณเก็บเงินฉันไปสองครั้งเลยนะ

(*Khun-kep-ngoen-chan-pai-song-khrang-loei-na*)

This item is damaged, I want to return it.

ของชิ้นนี้มีตำหนิ ฉันต้องการคืนของ

(Khong-chin-ni-mi-tam-ni-chan-tong-kan-khuen-khong)

I want to return this.

ฉันอยากเอาของนี่มาคืน

(Chan-yak-ao-khong-ni-ma-khuen)

I want to exchange this.

ฉันอยากเอาของนี่มาเปลี่ยน

(Chan-yak-ao-khong-ni-ma-plian)

Where is the supermarket?

ซุเปอร์มาร์เก็ตอยู่ตรงไหน

(*Supermarket-yu-trong-nai*)

What aisle is the fresh produce in?

ผักผลไม้สด อยู่ทางเดินไหน

(Phak-phon-la-mai-sot-yu-thang-doen-nai)

Where is the check out counter?

จ่ายเงินตรงไหน

(*Chai-ngoen-trong-nai*)

Are you open on Sundays?

วันอาทิตย์เปิดไหม

(Wan-a-thit-poet-mai)

Can you give me a cost estimate?
ราคาประมาณเท่าไร

(Ra-kha-pra-man-thao-rai)

That's too much
นั่นมันมากเกิน

(Nan-man-mak-koen)

Take it or leave it.
ซื้อไม่ก็ไปซะ

(*Sue-mai-ko-pai-sa*)

I'll give you five euros
ฉันจ่ายให้ห้ายูโร

(Chan-chai-hai-ha-yu-ro)

I'll give you eight euros for these two
ฉันให้แปดยูโรสำหรับสองชิ้นนี้

(Chan-hai-paet-yu-ro-sam-rap-song-chin-ni)

It's a real bargain
ราคาถูกมากๆ

(Ra-kha –thuk-mak-mak)

What a rip off

ราคาแพงมากๆ

(Ra-kha –phaeng-mak-mak)

Dating & Personal – การเดท และ เรื่องของบุคคล – Kan-det-lae-rueang-khong-buk-khon

To flirt

จีบ

(Chip)

Do you have a lighter?

มีไฟแช็คไหม

(Mi-fai-chaek-mai)

Do you have a cigarette?

มีบุหรี่ไหม

(Mi-bu-ri-mai)

I don't smoke

ฉันไม่สูบบุหรี่

(Chan-mai-sup-bu-ri)

You're pretty

คุณน่ารักจัง

(Khun-na-rak-chang)

You're beautiful

คุณสวยจัง

(Khun-suai-chang)

That's so cheesy!

น้ำเน่าจริงๆ

(Nam-nao-ching-ching)

I find you interesting

ฉันว่าคุณน่าสนใจจริงๆ

(Chan-wa-khun-na-son-chai-ching-ching)

Would you like to go out with me?

เป็นแฟนกันไหม

(Pen-faen-kan-mai)

I'll pick you up at 8

เดี๋ยวสองทุ่มมารับ

(Diao-song-thum-ma-rap)

I've reserved a table.

ฉันจองโต๊ะไว้แล้ว

(Chan-chong-to-wa-laeo)

This rounds on me.

ฉันเลี้ยงเอง

(Chan-liang-eng)

Let me buy you a drink.

ขอผมเลี้ยงเครื่องดื่มสักแก้ว

(Kho-phom-liang-khrueang-duem-sak-kaeo)

Can I buy you a drink?

ขอผมเลี้ยงเครื่องดื่มสักแก้วได้ไหม

(Kho-phom-liang-khrueang-duem-sak-kaeo-dai-mai)

May I join you?

ขอนั่งด้วยได้ไหม

(Kho-nang-duai-dai-mai)

Are you from around here?

คุณอยู่แถวนี้หรอ

(Khun-yu-thaeo-ni-ro)

I'm from London.
ฉันมาจากลอนดอน
(Chan-ma-chak-lon-don)

What do you do?
คุณทำงานอะไร
(Khun-tham-ngan-a-rai)

I'm a teacher.
ผมเป็นครู
(Phom-pen-khru)

Did you study at university?
คุณเรียนหนังสือที่มหาวิทยาลัยหรือเปล่า
(Khun-rian-nang-sue-thi-ma-ha-wit-tha-ya-lai-rue-plao)

I studied French
ฉันเรียนภาษาฝรั่งเศษ
(Chan-rian-pha-sa-fa-rang-set)

What are you studying?
คุณเรียนอะไร
(Khun-rian-a-rai)

I'm studying architecture

ฉันเรียนสถาปัตยกรรม

(Chan-rian-sa-tha-pat-ta-ya-kam)

Do you have a boyfriend?

คุณมีแฟนไหม

(Khun-mi-faen-mai)

Do you have a girlfriend?

คุณมีแฟนไหม

(Khun-mi-faen-mai)

To be engaged

หมั้น

(Man)

Are you married?

คุณแต่งงานหรือยัง

(Khun-taeng-ngan-rue-yang)

Yes, I'm married.

ฉันแต่งงานแล้ว

(Chan-taeng-ngan-laeo)

m single

นโสด

Chan-sot)

Do you have kids?

คุณมีลูกไหม

Khun-mi-luk-mai)

Yes, I have two kids

ฉันมีลูกสองคน

(Chan-mi-luk-song-khon)

Do you have any siblings?

คุณมีพี่น้องไหม

(Khun-mi-phi-nong-mai)

Yes, I have a brother and a sister

ฉันมีพี่ชาย/น้องชายคนและพี่สาว/น้องสาวคน

(Chan-mi-phi-chai/nong-chai-khon-lae-phi-sao/-nong-sao-khon)

I'm an only child

ฉันเป็นลูกคนเดียว

(Chan-pen-luk-khon-diao)

Do you like dancing?

คุณชอบเต้นไหม

(Khun-chop-ten-mai)

I like dancing salsa

ฉันชอบเต้นซัลซ่า

(Chan-chop-ten-san-sa)

Do you like Spanish food?

คุณชอบอาหารสเปนไหม

(Khun-chop-a-han-sa-pen-mai)

I love Portuguese food

ฉันรักอาหารโปรตุเกส

(Chan-rak-a-han-pro-tu-ket)

What music do you like?

คุณชอบเพลงแบบไหน

(Khun-chop-phleng-baep-nai)

like hip hop

ฉันชอบเพลงฮิปฮอป

(Chan-chop-phleng-hip-hop)

Do you like travelling?

คุณชอบท่องเที่ยวไหม

(Khun-chop-thong-thiao-mai)

Where have you travelled to?

คุณเคยไปเที่ยวที่ไหนบ้าง

(Khun-khoei-pai-thiao-thi-nai-bang)

Have you been to Barcelona?

คุณเคยไปบาเซโลน่าไหม

(Khun- khoei-pai-ba-se-lo-na-mai)

I love being with you

ฉันชอบอยู่กับคุณจริงๆ

(Chan-chop-yu-kap-khun-ching-ching)

It's been a delightful evening

เป็นค่ำคืนที่มีความสุขเหลือเกิน

(Pen-kham-khuen-thi-mi-khwam-suk-luea-koen)

I had a wonderful time

ฉันมีช่วงเวลาที่แสนวิเศษ

(Chan-mi-chuang-we-la-thi-saen-wi-set)

Do you live nearby?

คุณพักอยู่แถวนี้หรือเปล่า

(Khun-phak-yu-thaeo-ni-rue-plao)

I live in the centre

ฉันพักอยู่ใจกลางเมือง

(Chan-phak-yu-chai-klang-mueang)

I live nearby

ฉันพักอยู่แถวนี้

(Chan-phak-yu-thaeo-ni)

...ive far away

พักอยู่ไกลมาก

(...han-phak-yu-kai-mak)

...hall we split the bill?

...าแยกกันจ่ายไหม

(...ao-yaek-kan-chai-mai)

...hall we go dutch?

...าแยกกันจ่ายไหม

(...ao-yaek-kan-chai-mai)

My treat!

ฉันเลี้ยง

(Chan-liang)

Shall I drop you off at home?

ฉันไปส่งบ้านไหม

(Chan-pai-song-ban-mai)

Let me walk you home

ให้ฉันเดินไปส่งบ้านนะ

(Hai-chan-doen-pai-song-ban-na)

Do you want to come back to mine?

ไปบ้านฉันไหม

(Pai-ban-chan-mai)

I can't take my eyes off you

ฉันละสายตาจากคุณไม่ได้เลย

(Chan-la-sai-ta-chak-khun-mai-dai-loei)

You turn me on

คุณทำฉันใจเต้นแรง

(Khun-tham-chan-chai-ten-raeng)

Do you have a condom?

คุณมีถุงยางไหม

(Khun-mi-thung-yang-mai)

To date/go out with someone

ออกเดท

(Ok-det)

To cheat

นอกใจ

(Nok-chai)

Third Wheel

เป็นก้างขวางคอ

(Pen-kang-khwang-kho)

To make out

จูบ

(Chup)

One-night stand

อยู่กินกันคืนเดียว

(Yukin-kan-khuen-diao)

To have a one-night stand

ไปอยู่กินกันหนึ่งคืน

(Pai-yu-kin-kan-nueng-khuen)

To be in a relationship with someone

มีความสัมพันธ์กับใครบางคน

(Mi-khwam-sam-phan-kap-khrai-bang-khon)

Conclusion

Once you have tried out these phrases and had a look over them the next step is to practice, practice, and practice some more.

Begin by writing down the phrases you think will be most relevant to you and any that stick out to you as interesting. Write them down a few times by hand and get a feel for them, try saying them to yourself and consider looking up videos online that will give you a good idea of the pronunciation. Break them down into the components that work for you.

If you really want to nail the phrases then record yourself saying them and play your version next to the official one.

Try to have a few words and phrases ready that you can easily back up with hand gestures. For example certain meals, directions for taxi drivers, and numbers are good to have ready. If you count to three and show it with your fingers to a local they can help you with your pronunciation much quicker.

This is where you are going to get the most help and the most use out of your phrases: when speaking to locals. It's only by speaking in person that you can see if others can understand you and it's the best way to be nudged in the right direction. Try to take the time to really listen to what they say. If you can, ask them to break down things slowly into components you can echo back.

When trying out phrases use them in sensible situations so you don't have bad experiences. If someone looks like they are in a rush then avoid stopping them in the street and trying out your Thai because they might be dismissive of your attempts to speak Thai. Instead speak to people that are more relaxed –especially when you are speaking to someone with relatively good English that is happy to have a conversation.

Don't worry about sounding off or not getting the right pronunciation. The only way you'll learn is by trying to get it right and you should see it as a fun experience. You are in Thailand to enjoy everything the culture has to offer and there's no need to be bashful. You have probably had experiences with others that don't speak English that well; did you find yourself judging them or feeling annoyed?

Most likely you took the time to help them as best you could and were touched they were trying to get in touch with your culture. Those you meet in Thailand will likely be no different and an important part of Thai culture is respect and politeness. There is also not the same expectation that you learn or speak Thai while there, so the gesture of trying will be felt even stronger.

You'll find that outside a big city like Bangkok people in Thailand are often more relaxed and easy-going. Stopping to chat, even with a stranger, is seen as something that is worthwhile doing and there is not quite the same attitude that time is money.

Make sure to take part in activities where talking to local Thai people will be easy. Having a massage is a great opportunity to try your Thai phrases in a relaxed environment. With massages being available nearly everywhere you go for a few dollars there's no reason to not have them regularly either.

try to speak to a wide variety of people during your time in Thailand, you may find that some of the best impromptu language instructors are not students or tour guides, but monks, children, or old women on a quiet evening stroll.

You don't have to wait until you are in Thailand to try out your phrases either. You can start by slipping in a few Thai phrases in regular life – give a 'sawatdee' (hello) to your friends and family. If you live near a Thai restaurant or food supply store consider trying out a few choice phrases if you know the staff are from Thailand.

This phrasebook is an excellent tool to have for a quick reference or to look at when you are on the frontline in Thailand, but there's no reason you can't also pick up some more Thai learning materials before you go that will give you the basic building blocks as well. Consider trying out reading books for Thai children as often this is the best way to learn the basics.

You might want to find a language partner to help you learn. You could either find a Thai person in your area or online that wants to learn English and trade skills. Or you might just have a friend that wants to learn some basic Thai or is going to Thailand with you, and you can practice together.

There are enormous Thai language communities online and many of them are expats that are more than happy to help you in your quest to deliver some phrases in perfect Thai.

If you are interested you might want to start looking into different Thai arts and entertainment before you go. Some Thai music might not appeal to many westerners, especially if you don't like more traditional folk-style music, but the country puts out plenty of pop and rock music that can help you to start thinking in Thai. Often these groups will sing in Thai and English. If you get the chance to listen to an online Thai radio station that plays a mix of English and Thai music so you can pick up on common phrases.

Thailand has an interesting film scene, you'll find endless Muay Thai kickboxing films, but also some highly regarded and critically acclaimed dramas from directors such as Apichatpong Weerasethakul. These films are worth watching if you are just a cinema-nut, but by listening carefully and paying attention to the subtitles they can really help with your pronunciation.

While doing all of these be sure to create a cheat sheet for yourself where you write down phrases as you hear them and break them down into phonetic bites that work for you.

With a little bit of practice and a real attempt to go out among the people and use these phrases you should have great success and a lot of fun during your travels and adventures in Thailand.

Made in the USA
Columbia, SC
13 June 2021